Coping *with* Everyday Stressors *workbook*

Facilitator Reproducible Guided Self-Exploration Activities

Ester R. A. Leutenberg
& John J Liptak, Ed. D.

WholePerson
Mental Health & Wellness
publisher of therapy, counseling, and self-help resources

Whole Person Associates

101 West 2nd Street, Suite 203
Duluth, MN 55802

800-247-6789

Books@WholePerson com
WholePerson com

Coping with Everyday Stressors Workbook
Facilitator Reproducible Guided Self-Exploration Activities

Printed in the United States of America

Editorial Director: Carlene Sippola
Art Director: Joy Morgan Dey

Library of Congress Control Number: 2013954257
ISBN: 978-1-57025-305-8

Using This Book

In our frenetic society with demands being placed upon people in the workplace, school, community, and home, it is more important than ever for people to find creative ways to cope with and maybe even eliminate distress in their lives.

Distress is different than eustress (a name for good stress), which is the helpful type of stress, one that is a burst of energy, telling one's body what to do. It is the type of stress that can help one accomplish tasks, goals and projects, motivating one to move forward. Eustress becomes distress when it is overdone.

In this workbook, we will look at the four prominent dimensions which make up a sense of optimal wellness and help your clients experience Eustress, rather than distress, in their lives.

Dimensions

Emotional – Emotional wellness is a deep sense of happiness that comes from understanding personal own feelings and the feelings of other people, accepting personal strengths and weaknesses, and attaining a sense of emotional stability. It is also the ability to maintain effective personal and interpersonal relationships with others. Emotional wellness is the ability to express feelings in an appropriate manner, adjust well to change, and cope with life despite its frustrations and disappointments.

Cognitive – Cognitive wellness encompasses the ability to think clearly and creatively, willingness to continue learning throughout life, ability to apply the things learned in a variety of settings, and readiness to engage one's mind in interactions with the world. People who are cognitively well are able to absorb new ideas and concepts, understand how thinking affects behavior and emotional reactions, and are to remain steadfast in the face of challenges.

Physical – Physical wellness is associated with living a healthy lifestyle and includes eating a well-balanced diet, sleeping enough, engaging in plenty of physical activity and exercise, maintaining proper weight, and restricting intake of harmful substances such as alcohol, tobacco, drugs, and caffeine. Physical wellness encompasses taking measures to protect one's physical health, protect against illness and disease, and remain active throughout the lifespan.

Social – Social wellness is the ability to feel at ease and comfortable with oneself and with others. It is the ability to relate well to other people, be outgoing and friendly, and develop and maintain intimacy. Social wellness means one has the ability to handle conflicts while being true to one's own ideals and beliefs. It is being tolerant of others, especially those who are different. Social wellness means loving oneself in order to be able to love others.

(Continued on the next page)

Sources

We live in a world fraught with stress. Stress has many sources and can be generated from within a person through self-imposed thoughts and feelings, while others stressors come from the environment:

Stress generated from within a person - Stress can be self-imposed through low self-esteem, anger, feelings of hopelessness, feelings of helplessness, anxiety, perfectionistic tendencies, jealousy and hostility. For example, people who are perfectionistic often bring stress upon themselves by being too careful and worrying about tasks being perfectly accomplished.

Stress generated from the environment – Stress can be felt from the results of environmental catastrophes such as severe storms, earthquakes, tornadoes, hurricanes, floods and acts of war. For example, people who are trying to rebuild their homes and lives after a hurricane find themselves struggling to meet their most basic needs.

Stress generated from conflicts – Stress can be the result of situations in which people are faced with an incompatibility with people, needs, demands, opportunities or goals. For example, a person who does not get along with a co-worker will experience stress on the job.

Stress generated from daily hassles – Stress can be the result of minor irritating annoyances that occur in daily life. Some of these daily hassles may be losing keys, car breaking down, waiting in long lines at a store, waiting for appointments, and getting stuck in traffic. For example, a person having to sit in traffic going to and coming home from work will experience stress.

Stress generated from economic factors – Stress can be the result of economic factors such as losing money in the stock market, not having enough money in retirement, growing inflation, and amassing too much debt. For example, many people have to work later in life because of a lack of enough money to live on in retirement. People may struggle with overcrowded housing, inadequate heating or air-conditioning, dangerous neighborhoods, etc.

Stress generated from changes in families – Stress can be the results of changes in the family such as parents' separation, divorce, blended families, loss of loved ones, change in residence, birth of a child, adoption, changes in health of family members, and caring for aging parents. For example, people who are forced to care for aging parents often feel guilt, and are stressed because it takes time away from work and other family obligations.

Stress generated from changes at work – Stress can be the result of changes on a job, loss of work, changes in a role played at work, uncomfortable physical demands in the workplace, a lack of safety, interpersonal demands such as an abrasive supervisor or co-worker, and having too much work to complete. For example, a person who must work with an abrasive supervisor will feel uncomfortable most of the work day.

In order to successfully deal with all of the various types of stress, people must find creative ways of coping. The *Coping with Everyday Stressors Workbook* provides assessments and self-guided activities to help participants learn useful skills for coping creatively with the various forms of stress. Many choices of self-exploration activities are provided for participants to determine which best suit their unique needs.

Format of Book

The *Coping with Everyday Stressors Workbook* contains assessments and guided self-exploration activities that can be used with a variety of populations to help participants cope more effectively with the stressors and hassles in their lives. Each chapter of this workbook begins with an annotated Table of Contents with notes and examples for the facilitator. Each chapter contains two primary elements: 1) a set of assessments to help participants gather information about themselves in a focused situation, and 2) a set of guided self-exploration activities to help participants process information and learn ways of coping with stress.

Assessments

Each chapter begins with an assessment that provides participants with valuable information about themselves. These assessments help identify patterns of behavior and life skills which are productive and unproductive, and encourage development of an awareness of ways to interact with the world. Assessments provide a path to self-discovery through participants' exploration of their own unique traits and behaviors. The purpose of these assessments is not to "pigeon-hole" people, but to allow them to explore various elements that are critical for coping with everyday stressors and hassles. This workbook contains *self-assessments*, not *tests*. Traditional tests measure knowledge or right or wrong responses. For the assessments provided in this workbook, remind participants that there are no right or wrong answers. These assessments ask only for opinions or attitudes about topics related to a variety of coping skills and abilities.

The assessments in this book are based on self-reported data. In other words, the accuracy and usefulness of the information is dependent on the information that participants honestly provide about themselves. All of the assessments in this workbook are designed to be administered, scored, and interpreted by the participants as a starting point for them to begin to learn more about themselves and their coping skills. Remind participants that the assessments are exploratory exercises and not a final determination of abilities. Lastly, the assessments are not a substitute for professional assistance. If you feel any of your participants need more assistance than you can provide, please refer them to an appropriate professional.

As your participants begin the assessments in this workbook give these instructions:

- Because there is no time limit for completing the assessments, work at your own pace. Allow yourself time to reflect on your results and how they compare to what you already know about yourself.
- Do not answer the assessments as you think others would like you to answer them or how you think others see you. These assessments are for you to reflect on your life and explore some of the barriers that are keeping you from living a calmer, more rational and less anxious life.
- Assessments are powerful tools if you are honest with yourself. Take your time and be truthful in your responses so that your results are an honest reflection of *you*. Your level of commitment in completing the assessments honestly will determine how much you learn about yourself.
- Before completing each assessment, be sure to read the instructions. The assessments have similar formats, but they have different scales, responses, scoring instructions and methods for interpretation.
- Finally, remember that learning about yourself should be a positive and motivating experience. Don't stress about taking the assessments or discovering your results. Just respond honestly and learn as much about yourself as you can.

(Continued on the next page)

Format of Book *(Continued)*

Guided Self-Exploration Activities

Guided self-exploration activities assist participants in self-reflection and enhance self-knowledge, identify potential ineffective behaviors, and teach more effective ways of coping. Guided self-exploration is designed to help participants make a series of discoveries that lead to increased social and emotional competencies, as well as to serve as an energizing way to help participants grow personally and professionally. These brief, easy-to-use self-reflection tools are designed to promote insight and self-growth.

Many different types of guided self-exploration activities are provided for you to pick and chose the activities most needed by your participants and that will be most appealing to them.

The unique features of self-guided exploration activities make them usable and appropriate for a variety of individual sessions and group sessions.

Features of Guided Self-Exploration Activities

Quick, easy and rewarding to use – These guided self-exploration activities are designed to be an efficient, appealing method for motivating participants to explore information about themselves - including their thoughts, feelings, and behaviors - in a relatively short period of time.

Reproducible – Because the guided self-exploration activities can be reproduced by the facilitator, no more than the one book needs to be purchased. You may photocopy as many items as you wish for your participants. If you want to add or delete words on a page, make one photocopy, white out and/or write your own words, and then make photocopies from your personalized master.

Participative – These guided self-exploration activities help people to quickly focus their attention, aid them in the self-reflection process, and help them to learn new and more effective ways of coping.

Motivating to complete – The guided self-exploration activities are designed to be an energizing way for participants to engage in self-reflection and learn about themselves. Various activities are included to enhance the learning process related to developing important social and emotional competency skills.

Low risk – The guided self-exploration activities are designed to be less risky than formal assessments and structured exercises. They are user-friendly, and participants will generally feel rewarded and motivated after completing these activities.

Adaptable to a variety of populations – The guided self-exploration activities can be used with many different populations and can be tailored to meet the needs of the specific population with whom you work.

Focused – Each guided self-exploration activity is designed to focus on a single coping issue, thus enhancing the experience for participants.

Flexible – The guided self-exploration activities are flexible and can be used independently or to supplement other types of interventions.

Chapter Elements

The *Coping with Everyday Stressors Workbook* is designed to be used either independently or as part of an integrated curriculum. You may administer any of the assessments and the guided self-exploration activities to an individual or a group with whom you are working, or you may administer any of the activities over one or more days. Feel free to pick and choose those assessments and activities that best fit the outcomes you desire.

The first page of each chapter begins with a Table of Contents annotated with ideas and examples for the facilitator.

Assessments – Assessments with scoring directions and interpretation materials begin each chapter. The authors recommend that you begin presenting each topic by asking participants to complete the assessment. Facilitators can choose one or more, or all of the activities relevant to their participants' specific needs and concerns.

Guided Self-Exploration Activities – Practical questions and activities to prompt self-reflection and promote self-understanding are included after each of the assessments. These questions and activities foster introspection and promote pro-social behaviors and coping skills. The activities in this workbook are tied to the assessments so that you can identify and select activities quickly and easily.

The activities are divided into four chapters to help you identify and select assessments easily and quickly:

Chapter 1: Coping with Emotional Stress

This chapter helps participants identify the ways they can more effectively cope with stress through creative emotional stress management techniques.

Chapter 2: Coping with Cognitive Stress

This chapter helps participants identify the ways they can more effectively cope with stress through creative, cognitive stress management techniques.

Chapter 3: Coping with Physical Stress

This chapter helps participants identify the ways they can more effectively cope with stress through creative physical stress management techniques.

Chapter 4: Coping with Social Stress

This chapter helps participants identify the ways they can more effectively cope with stress through creative social stress management techniques.

Our thanks to these professionals who make us look good!

Art Director - Joy Dey

Editor and Lifelong Teacher - Eileen Regen

Editorial Director - Carlene Sippola

Proofreader - Jay Leutenberg

Reviewer - Carol Butler

Table of Contents

Coping with Emotional Stress

Coping with Cognitive Stress

Table of Contents *(Continued)*

Coping with Physical Stress

Coping with Social Stress

Coping With Emotional Stress

Table of Contents and Facilitator Notes

Table of Contents and Facilitator Notes

Ask the group for a show of hands of those who journal. Ask those who do journal if they find it satisfying and to talk about it. If no one finds journaling satisfying, ask why.

After handout is completed, ask if someone is willing to role play the situation indicated. If the situation involves others, ask them to go in a corner, rehearse it and then present it to the group.

Prior to distributing the handout, ask the group if they know people who think they are super-heroes who can do everything. Ask them to share why.

After the handout or mosaic is completed, ask participants if they are willing to share it with the group. You can let them decide if they wish to explain the various components of the mosaic.

After completing the handouts, ask participants if they found it easy or difficult to write this letter. If it was difficult, ask them to share why.

Prior to distributing handout, read the following to participants about the difference between distress and eustress. "Stress is a burst of energy, telling our body what to do. Eustress is another name for good stress, which is the helpful type of stress. Eustress becomes distress when it is overdone. Eustress is the type of stress that can help you accomplish good things in your life. It can be a factor, motivating us to move forward, enjoy events, and accomplish actions that require some effort but provide satisfaction."

After completing the handouts, ask people to shout out the responses of each face, one by one. There are no right or wrong responses. Possibilities are:

1. Discouraged

2. Hostile

If participants can identify the feelings, lead applause for the person displaying the feeling. As an alternative activity, ask pairs of people to pick an emotion cut-out from a container and role-model a situation involving the emotion.

Coping With Emotional Stress Scale Introduction and Directions

Maintaining your emotional wellness is critical in living a stress-free life. Emotional wellness includes awareness of your emotions at any given time, the ability to maintain an even emotional state regardless of what is happening around you, and the ability to control your emotions.

This assessment contains 20 statements related to your emotional wellness. Read each of the statements and decide whether or not the statement describes you. If the statement *does* describe you, circle the number under the TRUE column next to that item. If the statement *does not* describe you, circle the number under the FALSE column next to that item.

In the following example, the circled number under "TRUE" indicates the statement is descriptive of the person completing the inventory.

	TRUE	FALSE
I have difficulty identifying my feelings	(1)	2

This is not a test. Since there are no right or wrong answers, do not spend too much time thinking about your answers. Be sure to respond to every statement.

Turn to the next page and begin.

Coping With Emotional Stress Scale

	TRUE	FALSE
I have difficulty identifying my feelings	1	2
I have fairly consistent emotional states	2	1
I usually understand how others are feeling	2	1
I am able to maintain intimate relationships with others	2	1
I often am unable to express my emotions clearly	1	2
I adjust to change and cope with the stress of daily life	2	1
I tend to be positive most of the time	2	1
I have inner peace and contentment	2	1
Minor setbacks cause me stress	1	2
I don't waste time or energy dwelling on the past	2	1
I am unable to stay focused on the present	1	2
I am aware of my personal limitations	2	1
I have a hard time valuing and accepting myself	1	2
I manage my emotions well	2	1
I am aware of how my negative emotions affect others	2	1
I worry a lot about failure	1	2
I find it easy to forgive others	2	1
I am not able to laugh at myself	1	2
I can appropriately express my feelings	2	1
I have a hard time accepting constructive criticism	1	2

TOTAL = _______________

Go to the Scoring Directions on the next page

Coping With Emotional Stress Scale Scoring Directions

The *Coping with Emotional Stress Scale* is designed to help you explore how well you are managing your emotions in this stress-filled society.

Add the numbers that you circled on the scale. This will allow you to get your Emotional Wellness score. You will get a total in the range from 20 to 40. Then, transfer this total to the space below:

EMOTIONAL WELLNESS TOTAL = __________

Profile Interpretation

Scale Score	Result	Indications
20 to 26	Low	Low scores indicate that you are rarely able to manage your emotions well. Complete the following exercises to develop greater emotional wellness.
27 to 33	Moderate	Moderate scores indicate that you sometimes are able to manage your emotions well. Complete the following exercises to develop greater emotional wellness.
34 to 40	High	High scores indicate that you are pretty effective in managing your emotions. Complete the following exercises to develop greater emotional wellness.

Have a Good Laugh

Laughing and developing a good sense of humor can help you to effectively and creatively deal with the tension and stress in your life. There are several ways to bring laughter back into your life:

Wear a smile. Go ahead and try it right now. Put a big smile on your face. How do you feel?

____

____

____

What kind of reaction will you get from someone to whom you gave that smile?

____

____

____

Read a humorous book. What is the funniest book you have ever read?

____

____

____

Watch a funny movie. What are your favorite funny movies?

____

____

____

Talk with a friend who gives you a good laugh. Which friends make you laugh?

____

____

____

Recognize that there are situations that can be frustrating and stressful at the time, but when you look back at them, they can actually be seen as humorous. Name one of those situations.

____

____

____

Laughter is internal jogging. —Norman Cousins

A Positive Impact

By being useful to others you will feel good about yourself. Think about some of the projects for which you might volunteer. Some of the possibilities include volunteering to help animals, an elderly neighbor who can't go out, homeless populations, people incarcerated, people who have lost homes due to natural disasters, and people who need social support.

List some people whom you help, how they benefit, and how you benefit by helping them.

Person I Help	How This Person Benefits	How I Benefit

Now, identify some of the possible ways you would like to positively impact your community.

Person I Want To Help	Why I Want To Help This Person	What I Can Do To Help

Expressing My Feelings

**It is often healthy to express how you feel.
First, do so in the spaces that follow.**

Person To Whom I Want To Express My Feelings	What I Feel Towards This Person	Why?

Would it be helpful to actually express these feelings to any of these people? To whom?

____

____

____

How will you do it? In person? Letter? Email?

____

____

____

WHO Pushes Your Negative Emotional Buttons?

Who is it that pushes your emotional buttons?
How can you creatively avoid these people or better cope with them.
List the people who push your negative buttons, what they do, and how can you be more creative in coping with the situation.

Person Who Pushes My Negative Emotional Buttons	What This Person Does	How I Can Cope More Effectively

Of the above people you have listed, who may possibly have a positive impact on you, even though they push your negative emotional buttons. How?

(Continued on the next page)

WHAT Pushes Your Negative Emotional Buttons *(Continued)*

What situation pushes your negative emotional buttons?
How can you creatively avoid these situations or better cope with them.
List the situations that push your negative buttons, what happens, and how can you be more creative in coping with the situation.

Situations That Push My Negative Emotional Buttons	Why This Bothers Me	How I Can Cope More Effectively
1.		
2.		
3.		
4.		

What can you do ahead of time to avoid being in these situations?

1. ______________________________
2. ______________________________
3. ______________________________
4. ______________________________

What Am I Feeling?

In order to better manage your emotions, it is important to be able to recognize your feelings when they are occurring.

Below, begin to identify times, and possibly with whom, when you felt the various emotions.

Angry ______________________________

Apathetic ______________________________

Beautiful ______________________________

Bitter ______________________________

Bold ______________________________

Bored ______________________________

Embarrassed ______________________________

Empty ______________________________

Envious ______________________________

Frustrated ______________________________

Happy ______________________________

Horrible ______________________________

Inspired ______________________________

Mean ______________________________

Nasty ______________________________

Refreshed ______________________________

Safe ______________________________

Silly ______________________________

What did you learn about yourself and others from this exercise?

____

____

____

Acknowledging Feelings

It is important to face your feelings head on in order to deal with them effectively in the future. Often,when you are faced with a difficult or stressful situation, you react emotionally. You can actually choose how you will respond emotionally to most situations. This activity will show you how.

Recall a difficult or stressful situation from your past. Picture the situation as if you were watching it on television. Describe the situation:

____

____

____

How did you react emotionally? Describe your feelings.

____

____

____

What would have been a better response?

____

____

____

Now You Try!

Think about a difficult or stressful situation that is upcoming. Picture the situation as if you were watching it on television. Describe the situation:

____

____

____

How will you react emotionally? Describe your feelings.

____

____

____

Why will this be the best response?

____

____

____

Nature

Spending time in a wonderful natural setting can be very relaxing.
Your eyes will see the most healing colors of blue, green and brown.
You will hear the natural sounds of birds and streams.
You will smell the trees and the great outdoors.
For now, close your eyes and imagine a situation like this.
Imagine where you are, when, with whom and what you are doing.

Answer the following questions to identify places where you can get away and relax.

Where? ____

____

When? ____

____

Who are you with? ____

____

What are you doing? ____

____

____

____

____

____

____

What keeps you from enjoying nature? ____

____

____

____

____

____

My Strong Feelings

People experience strong emotions and it helps to understand what prompts these feelings. Below, list strong feelings you have had in the last month and what prompted them.

Strong Feelings	What I Was Doing	What I Was Thinking	How My Body Felt
1.			
2.			
3.			
4.			

In the above situations, how will you deal more effectively in the future?

1. ____

2. ____

3. ____

4. ____

My Stress Journal

A creative way to relieve stress through writing or drawing is to keep a journal. Journaling provides an outlet to express feelings and situations you may be hesitant to discuss aloud. It can give you ideas on how to deal with the problem now or in the future. If done well an entry in your journal can be a truly cathartic experience. By making an entry everyday about your inner most thoughts, daily struggles or major disappointments, you can work through the problem at hand and the way you feel about the problem.

Values of journaling:

- reduces stress
- heals
- helps you get to know and understand yourself better
- allows you to gain growth and maturity
- helps with problem-solving
- assists in decision making
- is a way to see things in a humorous way, especially when re-reading or reviewing it
- motivators
- has no rules – can be messy, poor grammar and/or spelled incorrectly
- improves trust in yourself
- allows you to listen to your inner-voice
- improves sensitivity
- teaches you how to share stories about your family and yourself

Each time you feel stressed-out, keep track of your feelings in your journal. As you keep a daily log, you will begin to see patterns and common themes.

Below, practice now, and then continue journaling tomorrow and each day after.

What caused a recent stress? Make a guess if you're unsure. ______________________________

____

How did you feel, both physically and emotionally? ______________________________

____

How did you act in response? ______________________________

____

What did you do to make yourself feel better? ______________________________

____

It's Rehearsal Time!

This technique can be effective in helping to reduce the stress of an upcoming event. For example, you may have a speech to give, a meeting that you dread, or a social activity that you are worried about.

By practicing the technique that follows, you can reduce the stress associated with future stressful events.

Picture and then write or draw about a future event that is causing you stress (bring as much detail as possible to the scene). By sharing it, you will make it real.

See yourself handling the situation calmly and confidently. Write or draw about how the successful handling of the situation will be.

Now, in your mind, begin to imagine yourself being successful. At the same time, rub your thumb and index finger together to form a cue that links the successful feeling and the cue. How does it feel?

As you enter the situation for real, use your cue of rubbing your thumb and index finger together to bring back the positive feelings and effective response in the current situation.

Shed Your Cape

Whether you realize it or not, you are not a superhero! This means you are an ordinary human being who can accomplish only so much.

What are some of the activities and tasks, you can shed, to be less like a superhero and more like the human you are.

What I Can Shed	What I Have to Do to Shed It	How I Will Benefit

What surprises you about what you wrote?

____

____

____

____

Mosaics

Mosaic is an art form which involves fitting small pieces of rock, shell, tile, or glass called tesserae together to create a pattern which may be abstract or representational. This craft can be used to decorate everything from chests of drawers to floors, and it has been a part of the artistic expression of many cultures all over the world.

In the space below, create your own mosaic.

My Love Letter or Poem

Write a poem or letter to yourself.
Often, we forget how we truly feel about ourselves.
Write about what you love about yourself and your life.

Dear ________________________________ ,

When I feel stressed, I will remember all that I love about myself and my life.

NAME

DATE

An Emotional Wellness Quotation

> *Stress is not what happens to us. It's our RESPONSE TO what happens.*
> *And RESPONSE is something we can choose.*
>
> ~ Maureen Killoran

What does this quote mean to you? ____________________

Why do you think Maureen Killoran says that stress is not what happens to us? ____________________

How does our response affect stress? ____________________

How can we choose how to feel in a stressful situation? ____________________

How does this quote relate to your life? ____________________

Noticing Feelings in Others

It is important to be able to notice the feelings other people are experiencing. This ability, referred to as empathy, is the ability to share other people's feelings.

Look at the following faces and determine what the person is experiencing. Write your response next to each picture.

1. ____________________

2. ____________________

3. ____________________

4. ____________________

5. ____________________

6. ____________________

7. ____________________

8. ____________________

Acting Out Your Feelings

The non-verbal awareness of your feelings (and the feelings of others) is critical in learning to deal with emotional stress.

For each of the following feelings, take one slip of paper and act out the feeling listed. See if other participants can identify the feeling.

Fear	Confusion
Anger	Pride
Sadness	Appreciation
Joy	Relaxed
Disgust	Disrespect
Surprise	Hopeful
Shame	Jealousy

Coping With Cognitive Stress

Table of Contents and Facilitator Notes

EXAMPLE:

Types of Pursuits	Describe What You Do	How It Helps You
Do word puzzles	*Complete the "Jumble" every day*	*Helps me to think logically*

EXAMPLE:

Types of Pursuits	Describe What You Do	How It Helps You
Scrapbooking	*Keep a scrapbook of my children's accomplishments*	*Helps me to remember*

Self-esteem is a key personal quality in maintaining cognitive wellness and in battling stress. In order to strengthen their self-esteem, ask participants to create and repeat self-statements. Ask participants to list aspects of themselves they feel good about such as these:

"I am a really special person with many gifts and talents."
"I like the person I am and I feel good about myself."
"I am unique in many ways including how I think, feel, and act."

For this activity, identify several blocks of time during the week for yourself to engage in fun activities you enjoy such as baking, learning, napping, writing or drawing in a journal, and gardening.

Remind participants that optimism is not inherited and it can be learned. Ask them to use the process for changing negative thoughts into positive ones. Ask for volunteers to share their reactions.

Tell participants to be as innovative as possible in creating their mind maps. Use colored pencils to help participants re-create emotional states.

Table of Contents and Facilitator Notes

Coping with Cognitive Stress Scale Introduction and Directions

Cognition deals with aspects related to how you think. Cognitive stress management techniques are based on the notion that the mind has a distinct influence on emotions and on the body, and therefore on health and wellness. People who are cognitively well are able to think clearly and actively engage in the world around them.

This assessment contains 20 statements related to your cognitive wellness. Read each of the statements and decide whether or not the statement describes you. If the statement does describe you, circle the number in the YES column next to that item. If the statement does not describe you, circle the number in the NO column next to that item. Do not pay attention to the numbers in the columns.

In the following example, the circled 1 indicates the statement does not describe the person completing the inventory:

	YES	NO
I am a curious person	2	(1)

This is not a test. Since there are no right or wrong answers, do not spend too much time thinking about your answers. Be sure to respond to every statement.

Turn to the next page and begin.

Coping With Cognitive Stress Scale

	YES	NO
I am a curious person	2	1
I am not very interested in continuing my education	1	2
I am able to apply what I have learned to my present life.	2	1
I rarely look for ways to learn more	1	2
I pick up new concepts quickly	2	1
I am not very creative.	1	2
I approach all tasks in the same manner	1	2
I rarely take the initiative in tasks available to me	1	2
I am bothered by unfamiliar situations	1	2
I seek personal growth by learning new skills	2	1
I have a good memory and use it to my advantage	2	1
I am always trying to improve myself	2	1
I consider myself a lifelong learner	2	1
I am intimidated by challenges	1	2
I look for ways to use my creativity	2	1
I am surrounded by optimistic people	2	1
I rarely set reasonable and small attainable goals for myself	1	2
I perceive challenges as a chance to learn	2	1
I am interested in causes beyond myself	2	1
I value myself as a person	2	1

TOTAL = ___________

Go to the Scoring Directions on the next page

Coping With Cognitive Stress Scale Scoring Directions

The assessment you just completed is designed to measure the extent of your cognitive wellness. For each of the items on the previous page count the scores you circled. Put that total on the line marked TOTAL at the end of the assessment.

Then, transfer your total to the space below:

Cognitive Wellness Total = __________

Profile Interpretation

Scale Score	Result	Indications
20 to 26	Low	Low scores indicate that you exhibit low cognitive wellness. Complete the following exercises to develop greater cognitive wellness.
27 to 33	Moderate	Moderate scores indicate that you exhibit average cognitive wellness. Complete the following exercises to develop greater cognitive wellness.
34 to 40	High	High scores indicate that you have good cognitive wellness. Complete the following exercises to develop even greater cognitive wellness.

Intellectual Curiosity

Cognitively well people work to stretch and challenge their minds with intellectual pursuits. What are some of the intellectual pursuits in which you are interested?

Types of Pursuits	Describe What You Do	Describe How It Helps You
Do word puzzles		
Read newspapers, magazines		
Socialize with thinking people		
Take classes		
Play chess and/or other games		
Read books		
Research online and/or in libraries		
Participate in and enjoy intellectual discussions		
Visit or volunteer at museums		
Other		
Other		

Creative Pursuits

Creative people work to stretch and challenge their minds with creative pursuits. What are some creative pursuits which interest you?

Types of Pursuits	Describe What You Do	Describe How It Helps You
Scrapbooking		
Draw, paint, sculpt		
Crafts (knitting, woodworking, sewing, making jewelry, etc.)		
Explore new recipes		
Surround yourself with creative people		
Theater		
Writing		
Music		
Photography		
Seek new challenges		
Other		

Mirror, Mirror

Self-esteem is a key personal quality for maintaining cognitive wellness and in battling stress. In order to strengthen your self-esteem, try creating and repeating *positive* self-statements, starting with I, in the spaces which follow.

Example:

"I am a very special person with many gifts and talents."

Now that you have created your list, say these positive self-affirmations in front of a mirror daily.

Time Blocking

When you feel rushed with more to do than you have time available, it is easy to feel overwhelmed. For this activity, identify several blocks of time during the week to set aside for yourself, to engage in fun activities you enjoy.

Day	Time I Can Block Off For Myself	Activities I Can Do In That Time
Monday		
Tuesday		
Wednesday		
Thursday		
Friday		
Saturday		
Sunday		

What will you need to do or change in order to have more time to enjoy your life?

___

___

___

You Can Become Optimistic!

Optimism is a learned, not an inherited, trait!
When we think negatively about ourselves, it heightens the stress in our lives.
One way to remain positive is to reflect on our thinking
and become aware of distorted thinking.

Let's look at the process for this.

Think about a situation when you were stressed.

____

____

____

What assumptions did you make about the situation?

____

____

____

What is a rational explanation for this situation?

____

____

____

Put the situation in perspective. How can the situation be viewed more rationally and positively, rather than emotionally?

____

____

____

What actions can you take rather than remaining stressed by the situation?

____

____

____

Mind Mapping

Mind Mapping is a process by which you use diagrams to outline information. With a mind map, you show ideas represented in your brain and map ideas together.

To begin your mind map, identify a situation that stresses you out and put that situation in the BLOCK in the middle. Then, in the CIRCLES around the block, add the people who are involved. Next, in the spaces next to the CIRCLES, add details about the situation. Last, on the lines around your mind map, write ideas about what you can do to feel less stressed in the situation.

Create a separate mind map for each stressful situation.

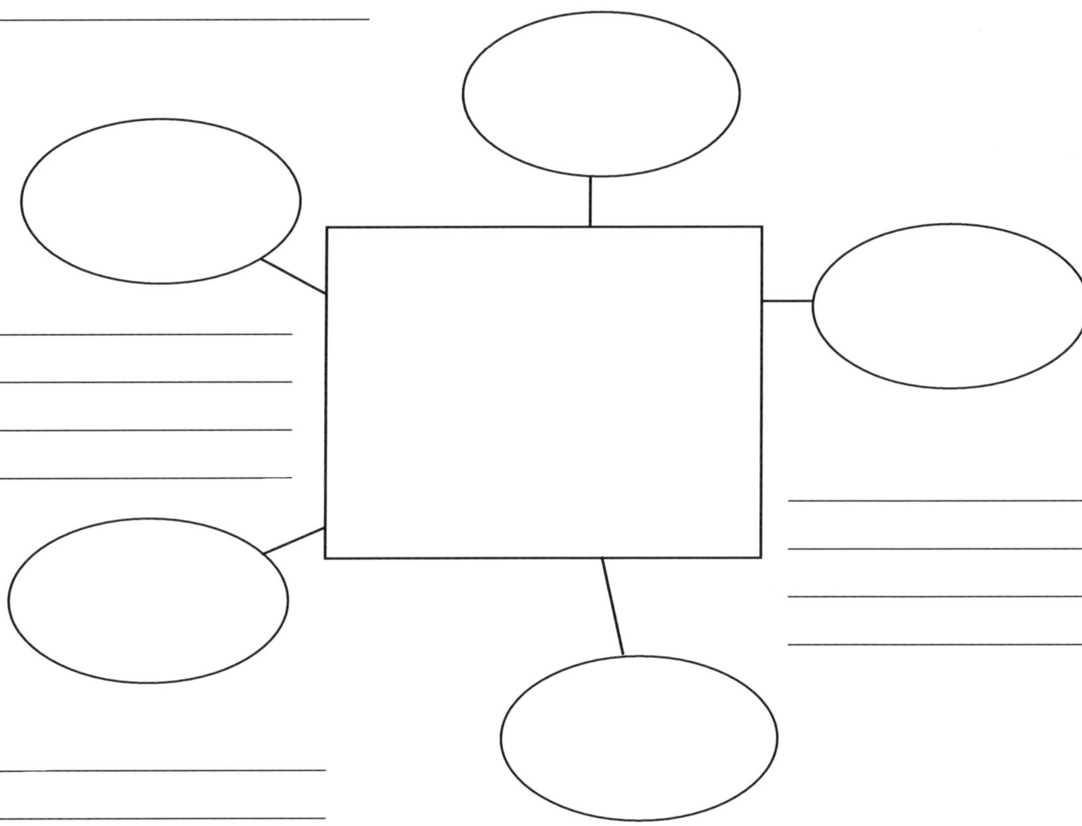

Self-Appreciation

Self-appreciation is the level of respect you have for your own value and significance. To maintain high cognitive wellness, determine what you appreciate about yourself.

Answer the following sentence prompts. Use specific details.

What I appreciate most about myself is ______________________________

____

____

What I appreciate most about my life is ______________________________

____

____

What I appreciate most about my personality is ______________________________

____

____

What I appreciate most about my body is ______________________________

____

____

What I appreciate most about my physical health is ______________________________

____

____

What I appreciate most about my emotional health is ______________________________

____

____

I appreciate my uniqueness in ______________________________

____

____

The talent I have which I appreciate most is ______________________________

____

____

The value that I most often display and that I appreciate the most is ______________________________

____

____

Other ______________________________

____

____

Get Involved

People who are cognitively well enjoy active participation in educational, cultural, and community activities outside of the classroom, home, workplace and/or volunteer job. These activities can provide respite from everyday stress. What types of educational, cultural and community activities do you enjoy?

Activity	Where I Engage In It	Why I Enjoy It

Now, think about the types of educational, cultural, and community activities you would like to join.

Activity	Where I Could Become Involved	Why I Would Enjoy It

See Life Differently

The next time you find yourself in a stressful or frustrating situation, try the following technique:

Become aware of times when you become angry, upset, frustrated or stressed. Write about the last time a stressful situation occurred. What was it?

____

____

____

Take a couple of deep breaths. Practice breathing in through your nose and letting your breath out through your mouth.

From your past, re-experience a positive event and the feeling associated with it. Think and write about a positive event from your past:

____

____

____

____

____

What feelings did you have when you recalled that positive experience?

- ❑ Love
- ❑ Devotion
- ❑ Compassion
- ❑ Exhilaration
- ❑ Patience
- ❑ Acceptance
- ❑ Appreciation
- ❑ Kindness
- ❑ Other ____________________
- ❑ Other ____________________

You can use this process to help you with any situation in the future.

Contemplation

Contemplation is meditation or deep reflection focused on important questions about life and yourself. This deliberate level of thinking can direct your mind to set aside the stress occurring in your life.

Who am I?

____

____

____

Why am I here?

____

____

____

Where do I come from?

____

____

____

What is the meaning of life for me?

____

____

____

What is the purpose of my life?

____

____

____

How can I live a more loving life?

____

____

____

Prioritize

With all you have to do, it is important to learn to prioritize what is important in your life.

For this activity, list ten tasks you have to do within the next week. Then in the right-hand column, place these tasks in order of importance with 1 being very important and 10 being least important.

____________	1	____________
____________	2	____________
____________	3	____________
____________	4	____________
____________	5	____________
____________	6	____________
____________	7	____________
____________	8	____________
____________	9	____________
____________	10	____________

What did you learn about yourself? ____________

What did you learn about your priorities? ____________

A Dale Carnegie Quotation

> *If we think happy thoughts, we will be happy.*
> *If we think miserable thoughts, we will be miserable.*
>
> — Dale Carnegie

What does this quote mean to you? ______________________________

What are some of your happy thoughts? ______________________________

What feelings do you experience when these thoughts occur? ______________________________

What types of miserable thoughts do you have? ______________________________

What feelings do you experience when these thoughts occur? ______________________________

Daydream

Many people find themselves involuntarily daydreaming when they feel bored or stressed. Daydreams can be your mind's way of escaping the stress of the moment. Giving yourself a mental break with a daydream is a quick way to step back from stressors and start fresh. What do you like to daydream about?

Write about or draw a representation of your most pleasant daydream.

Can you make it come true? How? If you can't, is it pleasant to think about?

Good Decision-Making

Part of cognitive wellness is the ability to make good choices and good decisions. In order to do this, use a process like the one below.

Step 1 – Identify the purpose of your decision. What is the decision you need to make?

Step 2 – Gather information for the various options you have available.

Step 3 – What will the likely results be for each option? Evaluate and rank each option from most likely to yield positive results to least likely to yield positive results.

Step 4 – Make a logical decision based on the information you have gathered.

Step 5 – Implement your decision.

Step 6 – Evaluate your decision.

Now you try. Think about an upcoming decision you are facing. Use the decision-making process outlined above to make an effective decision. Then use this process with all other decisions in your life.

Step 1 – Identify the purpose of your decision. What is the decision you need to make?

____

____

Step 2 – Gather information for the various options you have available. What information is available about your upcoming decision?

____

____

Step 3 – What will the likely results be for each option? Evaluate and rank your options from most likely to yield positive results to least likely to yield positive results.

____

____

Step 4 – Make a logical decision based on the information you have gathered. What is your decision?

____

____

Step 5 – Implement your decision. How will you make your decision a reality?

____

____

Step 6 – Evaluate your decision. What was the result of the decision you made?

____

____

New Skills to Master

One way that cognitively well people deal creatively with stress is by learning new skills. Learning new skills to master is a way of achieving personal growth. Think about some of the new skills you would like to master.

New Skill to Learn	How, Where or With Whom	Why I Want to Learn It

Rate the skills, number one being the skill you want to tackle first.

1. ____________________
2. ____________________
3. ____________________
4. ____________________
5. ____________________
6. ____________________
7. ____________________

Coping With Physical Stress

Table of Contents and Facilitator Notes

Prior to distributing handouts, ask for six volunteers. Each one will display one of the symptoms. Ask the group to guess the symptom that person is feeling.

Prior to distributing handouts, ask participants for a show of hands to indicate who likes to clean, straighten up, arrange drawers, work in the yard, etc., when feeling stressed.

Prior to distributing handouts, ask participants for a show of hands to indicate those . . .

- *who fall asleep almost as soon as their head hits the pillow.*
- *who are able to fall asleep in ten minutes or so.*
- *who can't fall asleep for hours.*
- *who fall asleep right away, but keep waking up.*

Prior to distributing handouts, define multi-taskers, who can do many things at one time, and tunnel people, who do or think about one thing at a time. Ask for a show of hands of multi-taskers and then of tunnel people.

Prior to distributing the handout, tell the participants that it is extremely important to listen to their body. Ask for volunteers to tell the group how they do that.

Prior to distributing the handout, explain to the group that smashing does not include people or anything valuable. (Pillows or punching bags are good to hit. An old dish is OK to smash somewhere safe. Stomping is okay if it is not hurtful to the body.)

Table of Contents and Facilitator Notes

Coping with Physical Stress Scale Introduction and Directions

Maintaining your physical wellness is critical in living a stress-free life. Physical wellness includes eating healthy meals and snacks, engaging in regular exercise and physical activity, and developing consistent sleep habits to help fight the effects of stress.

Read each statement carefully and decide if the statement applies to you always, sometimes or never. If it is always true for you, circle the number 3 next to the statement in that column. If it is sometimes true for you, circle the number 2 next to the statement in that column. If it is rarely or never true for you, circle the number 1 next to the statement in that column. Pay no attention to the numbers; read only the column headings. Complete all of the items before going back to score the assessment.

In the following example, the circled 2 indicates that the statement is Sometimes true for the person completing the scale.

	Always	Sometimes	Rarely or Never
I eat a well-balanced diet	3	(2)	1

This is not a test and there are no right or wrong answers. Do not spend too much time thinking about your answers. Your initial response will be the most true for you. Be sure to respond to every statement.

Turn to the next page and begin.

Name ______________________________ Date ________________

Coping with Physical Stress Scale

	Always	Sometimes	Rarely or Never
I eat a well-balanced diet	3	2	1
I have an active lifestyle	3	2	1
I have the energy to do things I like and need	3	2	1
I do not over-medicate myself	3	2	1
I engage in plenty of physical exercise and activity	3	2	1
I maintain a proper weight	3	2	1
I allow time for enough sleep each day	3	2	1
I avoid risky sexual behaviors	3	2	1
I refrain from using illegal drugs	3	2	1
I refrain from drinking alcohol	3	2	1
I refrain from using cigarettes, cigars, or smokeless tobacco	3	2	1
I take good care of myself if I become sick	3	2	1
I schedule regular physical examinations	3	2	1
I limit my exposure to the sun	3	2	1
I engage in aerobic exercises	3	2	1
I walk, jog or run regularly	3	2	1
I am satisfied with the condition of my health	3	2	1
I have a regular sleep routine	3	2	1
I enjoy yoga and other stretching exercises	3	2	1
I exercise through activities such as gardening	3	2	1

TOTAL = ______________________

Go to the Scoring Directions on the next page

Coping with Physical Stress Scale Scoring Directions

Look at the items you just completed. Add the numbers you circled on the scale and write that score on the line marked TOTAL. Then transfer that total to the space below:

PHYSICAL WELLNESS TOTAL = ________

Profile Interpretation

Scale Score	Result	Indications
20 to 39	Low	Low scores indicate that you are in poor physical wellness. Complete the following exercises to develop greater physical wellness.
40 to 49	Moderate	Moderate scores indicate that you are in fairly good physical wellness. Complete the following exercises to develop greater physical wellness.
50 to 60	High	High scores indicate that you have good physical wellness. Complete the following exercises to develop even greater physical wellness.

No matter how you scored, low, moderate or high, you will benefit from these exercises. By going to the next section and completing the activities that follow, you will greatly enhance your physical well-being.

Physical Distress Symptoms

How you move and hold your body tells a great deal about your level of stress and physical wellness.

Which of these physical distress symptoms do you exhibit and when do you find yourself experiencing them?

Physical Distress Symptom	When or With Whom Do You Find Yourself Displaying This Symptom?	What Can You Do to Overcome This?
Foot tapping (impatience)		
Tight, hunched shoulders (anxiety or frustration)		
Tightly folded arms (anger or disappointment)		
Sagging shoulders (fatigue)		
Biting nails (anxiety or worry)		
Frowning forehead (worry or fatigue)		
Clenched teeth (stressed)		
Biting or Licking Lips (nervousness)		
Downturned corners of mouth (disapproval)		
Other		
Other		

Cleaning

Cleaning is a way for many people to release anxiety. Repetitive movement can be relaxing and put you into a flow that resembles meditation.

Work around the house that would reduce my stress:

- ❑ Gardening
- ❑ Vacuuming / sweeping
- ❑ Washing windows
- ❑ Cleaning car
- ❑ Ironing
- ❑ Dusting
- ❑ Straightening out junk drawers
- ❑ Hiring a housekeeper
- ❑ Other:____________________
- ❑ Other:____________________
- ❑ Other:____________________
- ❑ Other:____________________
- ❑ Other:____________________
- ❑ Other:____________________
- ❑ Other:____________________
- ❑ Other:____________________

A drawer I would like to de-clutter is ____________________

Explain why ____________________

A room I would like to clean is ____________________

Explain why ____________________

A closet I would like to clean is ____________________

Explain why ____________________

Better Sleep Habits

Sleeping enough is critical in maintaining physical wellness as well as having the ability to cope with stress. With television, video games, computer games, books, etc., most people do not allow time for enough sleep and then feel even more stressed.

It is important to have a sleep routine so that you can be your best during the day.

How much sleep do you plan for each night?____________________

____

____

What interferes with your ability to sleep?____________________

____

____

What is your pre-sleep routine?__________________________

____

____

Does this routine help? _____________If so, how? ________________

____

____

If not, what can you do differently? ______________________

____

____

Which of the following could help you sleep better?

- ❑ Remove pets from the bedroom.
- ❑ Eliminate coffee or caffeinated soda and chocolate a few hours before bed.
- ❑ Engage in a relaxation activity.
- ❑ Take a hot shower or bath.
- ❑ Herbal tea.
- ❑ Listen to relaxing music.
- ❑ Remove the television from the bedroom.
- ❑ Prepare for the next day well before bedtime.
- ❑ Meditate.
- ❑ Write or draw in a journal.
- ❑ Read.
- ❑ Other:__________________________________ .

Healthy Lifestyle Activities

By putting yourself first, you can reduce the anxiety of juggling multiple roles through small acts of kindness toward yourself. Allow yourself to make time to nurture yourself.

Some nurturing activities are listed below. Place a check mark in the box in front of those you already do or plan to do and then list others on the blank lines.

- ❑ Take a walk
- ❑ Take a long bubble bath
- ❑ Go to a matinee movie
- ❑ Meditate
- ❑ Watch a sunrise or sunset
- ❑ Watch children play
- ❑ Plant a garden
- ❑ Listen to your favorite music
- ❑ Play with a pet
- ❑ Engage in yoga
- ❑ Curl up with a good book
- ❑ Take a camera walk through the park
- ❑ Bake bread from scratch, by hand
- ❑ ______________________________
- ❑ ______________________________
- ❑ ______________________________
- ❑ ______________________________
- ❑ ______________________________
- ❑ ______________________________
- ❑ ______________________________
- ❑ Schedule a massage
- ❑ Read an inspirational book
- ❑ Work on a crossword puzzle
- ❑ Write or draw in a journal
- ❑ Enjoy a local park
- ❑ Visit friends in person or by phone
- ❑ Rent and watch videos
- ❑ Browse in a bookstore
- ❑ Savor a cup of herbal tea or decaf coffee
- ❑ Visit a museum
- ❑ Take a class
- ❑ Play computer games
- ❑ Join a local sports team
- ❑ ______________________________
- ❑ ______________________________
- ❑ ______________________________
- ❑ ______________________________
- ❑ ______________________________
- ❑ ______________________________
- ❑ ______________________________

If My Body Could Talk

If your body could talk, what would it say?

For each of the statements below, write about what you think your body might say.

If my heart could talk, it would say…

If my arms could talk they would say…

If my lungs could talk, they would say…

If my legs could talk, they would say…

Smash Something

In Japan, a popular stress management technique is to smash plates. Taking out your frustrations and stress in a socially acceptable way can be effective in relieving the negative effects of stress. Think about things (not people) you have that you could hit, smash, or stomp.

Things I Could Hit	Things I Could Smash	Things I Could Stomp

Which do you think would relieve stress for you?

____

____

Which are you going to try first?

____

Unhealthy Eating Habits

Not eating properly can hinder your ability to effectively deal with stress. This assessment can help you determine if you are one of the three most prevalent types of psychological overeaters: night eaters, chronic dieters or binge eaters, or not.

	A Lot Like Me	A Little Like Me	Not Like Me
I skimp on meals to eat late at night.	3	2	1
I crave snacks at night.	3	2	1
I have trouble sleeping, so I eat.	3	2	1
I love to snack while watching television.	3	2	1
I like to eat more at night than during the day.	3	2	1

NIGHT EATER TOTAL = ___________

I try all of the latest diets.	3	2	1
After losing weight on a diet, I forget the diet and eat what I crave..	3	2	1
I overeat, and then crash diet before social events.	3	2	1
Weight-loss programs have failed me in the past.	3	2	1
I feel like I'm always watching what I eat.	3	2	1

CHRONIC DIETER TOTAL = ___________

I often eat uncontrollably.	3	2	1
I gobble food fast.	3	2	1
I eat when I'm upset.	3	2	1
I can easily eat a bag of my favorite snacks.	3	2	1
I eat huge amounts of food and feel powerless to stop.	3	2	1

BINGE EATER TOTAL = ___________

For the above assessment, add the number of the answers you circled and put that number on the line for your score. If your score is from 5-8, you do not show signs of these unhealthy eating habits. If your score is from 9-11, you have some of the signs of unhealthy traits. If your score is from 12-15, you have many of the signs of these eating habits. No matter how your score, you will benefit from the next exercises.

Healthy Eating

How can you eat healthier?

Place a check mark in front of the tips below that you will promise yourself to do.

- ❑ Cook wisely
- ❑ Read food labels
- ❑ Eat out less
- ❑ Eat a healthy breakfast
- ❑ Eat more, but smaller meals each day
- ❑ Plan meals ahead of time
- ❑ Shop sensibly
- ❑ Eat meals and snacks slower
- ❑ Avoid processed foods
- ❑ Eat smaller portions
- ❑ Eat at a table
- ❑ Do not watch TV or read while eating
- ❑ Avoid eating large snacks after dinner
- ❑ Don't let yourself get too hungry
- ❑ Drink a lot of water

Brainstorm with others additional ways that you can begin to develop a healthier eating plan for yourself and list them below:

____

____

____

____

____

____

____

____

____

____

____

____

____

____

____

Delegate

Delegating is assigning responsibility for a task to another person.
Delegating will free up time for you.
Look for ways to ask for others' help to keep you from feeling overloaded.

What I Want to Delegate	To Whom I Want to Delegate This Task	How This Will Help Me

Think about how you can delegate in a way that people will want, and be willing, to accept responsibilities.

____

____

____

Dance Your Stress Away

Dancing can be very relaxing and can be a way of reducing the stress in your life. There are people who live in very poor countries, yet they dance while working, relaxing, and communicating with friends and family.

How do you think dancing can help you reduce stress?

What types of dancing do you enjoy (belly, jazz, salsa, swing, zumba, etc.)?

What is a type of dance you would like to learn?

With whom do you like to dance? Why?

Where could you dance?

Are you willing to dance alone at home, or go out dancing alone? Why or why not?

Are you willing to go out dancing even if you don't know how? Why or why not?

Consequences of Role Overload

Juggling multiple roles can be both frustrating and stressful. When your demands exceed your inner resources for managing them, stress is the result.

Place a check mark in front of the roles that apply to you, and then describe how each role positively and negatively affects you.

✔	Roles I Play	How This Role Affects Me In a Positive Way	How This Role Affects Me In a Negative Way
	Partner		
	Parent		
	Son/ Daughter		
	Sibling		
	Grandparent		
	Other Relative		
	Friend		
	Neighbor		
	Employee/ Employer		
	Student		
	Volunteer/ Co-worker		
	Hobbyist		
	Neighbor		
	Other		
	Other		

Which roles cause you the most stress?

____

____

Physical Stress Signals

We all need to be more aware of how and when stress is affecting our physical wellness.

Place a check mark in front of the physical signals that you exhibit when you are stressed:

- ❑ A heavy feeling
- ❑ Chest pain
- ❑ Diarrhea or constipation
- ❑ Dizzy feelings
- ❑ Dry mouth
- ❑ Fatigue
- ❑ Flushed
- ❑ Headaches
- ❑ Loss of appetite
- ❑ Neck and /or back pain
- ❑ Pounding heart
- ❑ Sweaty hands
- ❑ Trembling / Twitching
- ❑ Upset stomach

Here is a brief relaxation technique that will quickly help to reduce stress on the spot. Set aside at least 15 minutes a day to relax, or use this the next time you feel the physical signals of stress.

1) Push your stomach out and draw a long, deep breath
2) Hold it for 3 seconds
3) Exhale a long breath, slowly
(as you exhale, let your shoulders drop and relax)
4) Allow the relaxation to flow
from your shoulders down your arms to your fingertips

Physical Activity

Physical activity can be an effective and an enjoyable way to reduce the stress in your life. Physical activity comes in a variety of forms. Think about how much physical activity you engage in.

Place a check mark in the boxes below to indicate which activities you currently engage in and then describe your involvement.

❑ Exercise ______________________________

____

❑ Walk / jog / walk a pet ______________________________

____

❑ Take the stairs instead of elevators ______________________________

____

❑ Park as far away from the door as possible ______________________________

____

❑ Play sports ______________________________

____

❑ Work around the house ______________________________

____

❑ Exercise / practice yoga, tai chi, etc. ______________________________

____

❑ Take Martial arts / dance classes ______________________________

____

❑ Meet with a personal trainer ______________________________

____

❑ Schedule fitness club workouts ______________________________

____

❑ Swim or water exercise ______________________________

____

❑ Ride a bicycle ______________________________

____

❑ Lift weights ______________________________

____

❑ Engage in aerobic activity ______________________________

____

❑ Stretch ______________________________

____

Which activities do you want to begin? ______________________________

____

____

My Sacred Space

It would be very helpful to set aside an area of your home or office where you can relax.

Where could this space be for you?

____

____

____

____

What do you imagine this space could look like and how might you make it attractive?

____

____

____

____

What could make it relaxing?

____

____

____

____

What personal items could you include in your space?

____

____

____

____

What ritual could you complete upon entering and/or leaving your space.

____

____

____

____

A Physical Stress Management Quotation

> *If your teeth are clenched and your fists are clenched,*
> *your lifespan is probably clenched.*
>
> — Adabella Radici

What does this quote mean to you? ______________________________

____

____

____

How do aspects of your body stay "clenched"? ______________________________

____

____

____

How can you begin to relax more? ______________________________

____

____

____

What techniques can you use to relax your muscles? ______________________________

____

____

____

How does this quote relate to your life? ______________________________

____

____

____

Coping With Social Stress

Table of Contents and Facilitator Notes

How I Can Contribute	How My Community Will Benefit	How I Will Benefit
Pick up litter by the river	*Will enhance the natural environment*	*Get me outdoors and be more active than I have been*

Support System	How This Person Buffers Me From Stress	How I Can Spend More Time With This Person
My sister	*I can talk to her about anything*	*Make a weekly standing date*

Provide some examples of the various ways people can be negative such as complainers, naysayers, and people who think that nothing can be done. Have participants identify negative people they know at home, in their community, or at work.

Comparing oneself to other people will make anyone negative. Help participants brainstorm ways of avoiding comparisons with others at home and/or at work.

Discuss the four primary ways people handle conflicts. After completing the handout, break participants into four groups based on their conflict-resolution styles. Ask them to describe how they would handle a conflict. Compare and contrast responses by each group.

Ask participants to pair up and practice their communication skills using the techniques described. One example of an I-Message is: "I feel hurt when no one asks what I want to do."

It is critical that social support be a two-way street. Ask participants to brainstorm ways they can be more supportive of others in their lives.

Participants think about the talents that they have, and describe how they could use them to help other people. For example, if they like baking, they can share some of their baked items with a neighbor.

Table of Contents and Facilitator Notes

Coping with Social Stress Scale Introduction and Directions

Social wellness is one's ability to effectively interact with people, use positive communication skills, have meaningful relationships with others, and create a social support system of friends and family.

The *Coping with Social Stress Scale* can help you explore the level of your social wellness. This assessment contains 20 statements. Read each of the statements and decide how descriptive the statement is of you. In each of the choices listed, circle the number of your response on the line to the right of each statement.

In the following example, the circled 1 indicates that the statement is not at all descriptive of the person completing the scale.

4 = Very Descriptive | **3 = Somewhat Descriptive** | **2 = A Little Descriptive** | **1 = Not At All Descriptive**

I am outgoing and affectionate toward others 4 3 2 (1)

This is not a test and there are no right or wrong answers. Do not spend too much time thinking about your answers. Your initial response will be the most true for you.
Be sure to respond to every statement.

Turn to the next page and begin.

Coping with Social Stress Scale

4 = Very Descriptive   3 = Somewhat Descriptive   2 = A Little Descriptive   1 = Not At All Descriptive

I am outgoing and affectionate toward others	4	3	2	1
I can balance my needs and the needs of others	4	3	2	1
I am concerned for the environment	4	3	2	1
I relate well to others in my family	4	3	2	1
I relate well to others in my community	4	3	2	1
I am tolerant of others	4	3	2	1
I tend to openly share my thoughts and feelings with others	4	3	2	1
I am able to develop and maintain intimacy	4	3	2	1
I am loyal and faithful to family members.	4	3	2	1
I treat others with respect and fairness	4	3	2	1
I like helping others	4	3	2	1
I have a network of friends and family	4	3	2	1
I find joy in working with others to accomplish tasks	4	3	2	1
I am rarely jealous of other people	4	3	2	1
I enjoy interacting with people from other cultures	4	3	2	1
I am a good listener	4	3	2	1
I am a good communicator	4	3	2	1
I am committed to the good of my community	4	3	2	1
I truly care about other people	4	3	2	1
I enjoy spending time with other people	4	3	2	1

TOTAL = ____________________

Go to the Scoring Directions on the next page

Coping with Social Stress Scale Scoring Directions

The assessment you just completed is designed to measure the extent of your social wellness. For each of the items on the previous pages, count the scores you circled. Put that total on the line marked TOTAL at the end of the assessment.

Then, transfer your total to the space below:

SOCIAL STRESS TOTAL = ___________

Profile Interpretation

Scale Score	Result	Indications
20 to 40	Low	Low scores indicate that you exhibit low social wellness. Complete the following exercises to develop greater social wellness.
41 to 60	Moderate	Moderate scores indicate that you exhibit average social wellness. Complete the following exercises to develop greater social wellness.
61 to 80	High	High scores indicate that you have good social wellness. Complete the following exercises to develop even greater social wellness.

Welfare of My Community

How can you better contribute to the welfare of your community?

How I Can Contribute	How My Community Will Benefit	How I Will Benefit

Which will you start immediately and why?

____

____

____

An Investment in Time

It is important to spend time with positive people. A strong support system will buffer you from the negative effects of stress. Who is in your support system and how does each person buffer you from stress?

Support System	How This Person Buffers Me From Stress	How Can I Spend More Time With This Person?

How can you be a better support to the people listed above so that they too do not experience as much stress?

___

___

___

___

Avoid Negative People

It is best to choose your friends carefully. When you are friends with people who have a negative attitude, you'll find yourself engaging in negative conversations which can zap your energy. Negative people can be at home, work, in your community – anywhere.

Negative Person	How This Person Affects Me	How I Can Change My Relationship With this Person

If you made changes in your relationship with any of the persons above, how would that change impact your life?

___

___

___

Stop the Comparisons!

You make your life more stressful when you compare your life to others.
With whom do you compare yourself at HOME?

People to Whom I Compare Myself	Why I Do It	How It Negatively Affects Me

With whom do you compare yourself at WORK?

People to Whom I Compare Myself	Why I Do It	How It Negatively Affects Me

Where do most of your comparisons occur? What can you do about it?

____

____

____

Live in Harmony

Conflicts occur in your life and add to the stress you experience.
The following assessment will help you determine your conflict management style.

When I am in conflict ...

I attempt to find a middle-ground	YES	NO
I give up some concerns and agree to concerns of the other person	YES	NO
I compromise so that we can still be friends	YES	NO
I give in a little to find a solution	YES	NO
I think hard about how important this situation and person is to me.	YES	NO

Compromise TOTAL = ________

When I am in conflict ...

I do not consider the point of view of the other person	YES	NO
I argue the merits of my position	YES	NO
I assert myself and do not bend	YES	NO
I enjoy debating the issue loudly	YES	NO
I stand my ground stubbornly throughout the process	YES	NO

Competition TOTAL = ________

When I am in conflict ...

I avoid the person entirely	YES	NO
I ignore the conflict until it goes away	YES	NO
I withdraw from the situation even though it hurts me to do so	YES	NO
I behave in a passive way	YES	NO
I let the situation resolve itself	YES	NO

Avoidance TOTAL = ________

When I am in conflict ...

I tell the person I agree even though I don't.	YES	NO
I ignore my own goals to resolve the conflict.	YES	NO
I try to accommodate the wishes of the other person	YES	NO
I give in to the needs of the other person, ignoring my own	YES	NO
I do what I need to do in order to keep the peace	YES	NO

Giving-In TOTAL = ________

To score this quick assessment, count the number of "YES" answers you circled for each of the styles. The style in which you had the highest total is your primary conflict management style.

If you scored high in two areas, you tend to use both when in a conflict.

The "Compromise" style is considered the best to maintain social wellness.

Communicate Thoughts, Ideas and Feelings

Most conflicts are the result of sending poor messages to other people. You can limit the intensity of your conflicts by sending good vibes and listening actively.

When you find yourself in a conflict, take responsibility for what you say:
Use words like I, me and my, to communicate your message. In this way you *"own"* the messages you send to them. Take responsibility for your own words. When you use words like *"they said"* or *"some people,"* you put the responsibility of what you are saying onto someone else. Using *"you"* often sounds threatening, aggressive and blaming, whereas creating I-messages conveys your comments in a positive way.

Maintain eye contact and speak directly to the person. Try not to stare, look away too often, cross your arms in front of you, or allow yourself to be distracted.

Now you try!
In the spaces that follow, note the people involved and provide some I-Statements.

People With Whom I Want To Communicate Better	Thoughts, Ideas and Feelings I Want To Communicate

My Social Network – Give & Take

Creating a support network is a basic building block in developing and maintaining social wellness. Think about your friends and family. Identify who makes up your social network.

Person In My Network and Relationship To Me	How This Person Supports Me	How I Support This Person

What did you learn from this activity?

____

____

____

____

Ways to Share My Talents

Being part of a community means sharing your gifts, talents, and natural abilities to help other people. Think about the talents that you have. Describe how you could use them to help other people.

My Talents	With Whom I'll Share	How I Will Share

Is there anyone with whom you use the "barter system" – a system in which you share your talents and receive something back in return, thus helping both of you? Describe.

____

____

____

Reach Out

Reaching out to others can be difficult but very rewarding.

How can you more effectively reach out to other people?

People I don't know and whom I would like to know, and why.

____

____

____

People I know a little and whom I would like to know better, and why.

____

____

____

People I wish to know better than I do already, and why.

____

____

____

People who have experienced hardships and whom I would like to help, and how I can help them.

____

____

____

People I can empower, and how I can do it.

____

____

____

Intentional Time

Dedicating intentional time to build relationships with family, friends and acquaintances is important in maintaining your social wellness. Below, identify times and ways you will connect or re-connect with significant people in your life.

People in My Life	When I Can Connect With These People	How I Will Connect With Them
Family		
Friends		
Acquaintances		
Co-workers		
Others		

Take Interest in Other People

How much do you really know about the people in your life? Taking interest in and learning about various people will add to your relationships and help to open your world.

Person in My Life	How I Know This Person	What I Want to Learn About This Person

Be a Social Butterfly

Socially-well people are able to develop relationships with other people based on mutual interests.

Identify your interests and ways that you can use those interests to develop more, or improve on, existing relationships.

My Interests	How I Will Use My Interest To Broaden and Improve My Friend-Base	What I Hope To Do

Describe your plan.

____

____

____

Take Interest in People Different From You

Think about all of the people you know who are different from you (religion, race, gender, age, etc.) What more would you like to know about these people?

Person	How This Person Is Different Than Me	What I Want To Know More About This Person

How can you go about finding out more about these people?

Practice Self-Disclosure

If you have people who are interested in you and want to learn more about you, it is healthy to disclose personal information about yourself without crossing over interpersonal boundaries.

Finish the following sentences related to self-disclosure.

I am ____ .

I was born ____ .

I have done ____ .

I wish I could ____ .

I am good at ____ .

I was born and raised in ____ .

When I was young, I ____ .

As a teen, I ____ .

My favorite color is ____ .

The work I do is ____ .

My dream job would be ____ .

I regret ____ .

My family was ____ .

The one thing I would change about myself is ____ .

My favorite movie is ____ .

My favorite music is ____ .

My favorite book is ____ .

My personality could be described as ____ .

My passion is ____ .

Only disclose information that you feel comfortable with everyone knowing. Do not disclose info that you wouldn't want everyone to know or repeat. Do any of the above responses provide more information that you would want everyone to know?

____

____

____

My Community Offers

What types of social activities are offered in your community? These social activities can be fun and serve as stress reducers.

Offered in My Community	Why it Sounds Good to Me	How I Can Get More Info.

Pay Attention

It is important to pay attention to people and listen carefully to assure that conflicts do not occur in your social life.

Here are some basic attention skills to utilize while communicating with other people. Try them with another person.

Use positive body language

- Face the other person
- Open your posture
- Present positive body language
- Lean slightly towards the person
- Maintain eye contact
- Relax while listening to the person
- Stay focused on the speaker
- Nod to suggest you understand what is being said
- Listen without interrupting

How did it feel to listen actively?

____

____

____

How can this help you with your social relationships?

____

____

____

Write about one of your relationships that would have benefitted by your paying attention.

____

____

____

Social Ladder

It can be challenging to risk developing and maintaining social relationships, or improving existing social relationships. It helps to build up to greater social risk-taking. It is a good idea to start slowly and build up to increased social interactions.

Answer the following questions at the bottom of the ladder and work your way up.

Whom can I invite to a community activity?

____

____

With whom can I go to a movie?

____

____

Whom can I ask to join me for dinner?

____

____

Who is someone for whom I can plan a social activity and invite others?

____

____

Whom can I call, email or text regularly, each week?

____

____

Who are five people I would like to have as better friends?

____

____

____

____

____

Be a Pillow

> *When tough times come,*
> *it is particularly important*
> *to offset them with*
> *much gentle softness.*
>
> *Be a pillow.*
>
> — Vera Nazarian

How can you be a pillow for a particular person you know who is going through a tough time?

Describe how a particular person has been your pillow.

Whole Person Associates is the leading publisher of training resources for professionals who empower people to create and maintain healthy lifestyles. Our creative resources will help you work effectively with your clients in the areas of stress management, wellness promotion, mental health and life skills.

Please visit us at our web site: **WholePerson.com**.You can check out our entire line of products, place an order, request our print catalog, and sign up for our monthly special notifications.

Whole Person Associates

800-247-6789